Learn Haskell

Practical Guide

A. De Quattro

Copyright © 2024

Guide to Haskell

1.Introduction

Haskell is a functional programming language that was developed in 1987 by a group of researchers led by Paul Hudak at Yale University. It is based on lambda calculus, a mathematical model that describes computation with functions. Haskell was designed to be an elegant and powerful programming language aimed at providing developers with a better way to write robust, modular, and maintainable software.

A unique aspect of Haskell is its strong and static type system, which allows developers to catch programming errors during the compilation phase rather than during program execution. This makes Haskell particularly suitable for writing critical software, where safety and reliability are of paramount importance. Another strength of Haskell is its expressiveness and conciseness. Thanks to its elegant and functional syntax, Haskell enables developers to write cleaner, clearer, and more readable code compared to other more traditional programming languages like Java or C++. Additionally, Haskell supports purely functional programming, allowing developers to write more robust and maintainable code through the use of pure functions and data immutability.

In this article, we will delve into the main concepts of Haskell, exploring its syntax, its distinctive features, and how to use it to write quality software.

Basic Syntax of Haskell

One of the first things you will notice in Haskell is that the syntax is very different from other more common programming languages like Java or C++. Haskell is a purely functional language, which means that everything in Haskell is a function, including arithmetic and logical operators. For example, to sum two numbers in Haskell, you use the function "+":

```
x = 5
y = 10
sum = x + y
```

In Haskell, functions are defined using the keyword "let" followed by the function name and its arguments. For example, to define a function that calculates the double of a number, you can do it like this:

```
double x = x * 2
```

This defines a function called "double" that

takes a single argument and returns the double of that number.

Functions in Haskell are also immutable, which means that once a variable has been assigned a value, it cannot be changed. This promotes safer programming and prevents common errors like simultaneous access to shared data.

Data Types in Haskell

Haskell is a strongly typed language, which means that every expression in Haskell has a defined type at compile time. This helps prevent common type errors and allows you to write more reliable code.

There are several basic types in Haskell, such as Int (for integers), Float (for floating-point numbers), Char (for characters), and Bool (for boolean values). Additionally, Haskell supports the creation of custom data types through the definition of new types and data structures.

For example, we can define a new data type called "Person" with the fields "name" and "age" as follows:

```
data Person = Person { name :: String, age :: Int }
```

This definition creates a new data type called "Person" with two fields, "name" of type String and "age" of type Int. This allows us to create instances of this data type and manipulate the data effectively.

Pattern Matching and Recursion

One of the most powerful features of Haskell is pattern matching, which allows you to break down complex data into smaller parts and treat them separately. This makes the code more readable and concise.

For example, we can define a function that calculates the factorial of a number using pattern matching:

```
factorial 0 = 1
factorial n = n * factorial (n-1)
```

In this example, if the argument "n" is equal to 0, then the factorial is 1. Otherwise, the factorial of "n" is given by "n * factorial (n-1)", which uses recursion to calculate the factorial of smaller numbers.

Recursion is a common technique in Haskell due to its functional and immutable nature. Recursion allows you to write more concise and elegant code compared to other more common iterative techniques.

Higher-Order Functions

Haskell supports higher-order functions, which are functions that take other functions as arguments or return other functions as results. This allows you to write more generic and reusable code, promoting modularity and function composition.

For example, we can define a function that takes another function as an argument and a value, and applies the function to the argument:

```
applyFunction :: (a -> b) -> a -> b

applyFunction f x = f x
```

This function takes two arguments, a function "f" that maps a value of type "a" to a value of type "b" and a value "x" of type "a". The output of the function is the result of applying the function "f" to the argument "x".

Higher-order functions are a powerful feature of Haskell that allows you to write generic code and reduce code duplication, promoting the reusability and maintainability of software.

Monad and IO

One of the most interesting features of Haskell is the use of monads to handle side effects and input/output operations. Monads are a data structure that represents a computation, allowing you to combine and sequence functional computations in an orderly and controlled manner.

In Haskell, the most common monad is the IO monad, which represents input/output operations such as reading from a file or interacting with the user. With the IO monad, we can write imperative code in a functional way and maintain the purity of the language.

For example, we can define a function that prints a message to the screen and reads an input from the user using the IO monad:

```
greet :: IO ()

greet = do

  putStrLn "Hello! What's your name?"
```

```
    name <- getLine

    putStrLn ("Welcome, " ++ name ++ "!")
```
```

In this example, the function "greet" uses the IO monad to print a welcome message, read an input from the user, and print another greeting message to the user.

Monads are an advanced feature of Haskell that allows you to elegantly and safely handle side effects in functional code.

Conclusion

Haskell offers concise and readable syntax, a strong and static type system, and supports purely functional programming.

With Haskell, you can write robust, modular,
```

and maintainable software thanks to its functional syntax and immutable nature. The use of techniques such as pattern matching, recursion, higher-order functions, and monads make Haskell a versatile language suitable for a wide range of applications.

2.Installation of Haskell

Haskell is a pure functional programming language known for its elegant syntax and powerful mechanisms for handling functions and complex data types. If you're interested in learning Haskell and starting to develop projects with this language, the first thing you need to do is install Haskell on your computer. In this article, I will guide you step by step through the process of installing Haskell on different operating systems.

Before we begin, it's important to note that there are different ways to install Haskell. One of the most common options is through GHC (Glasgow Haskell Compiler), the main Haskell compiler used by most developers. GHC also includes GHCi, an interactive interpreter for Haskell that allows you to write and execute Haskell code directly from the console.

Another option is to use Haskell Platform, a set of pre-installed tools and libraries for Haskell development. Haskell Platform includes GHC along with a range of popular and useful libraries for Haskell projects.

Regardless of the method you choose, the Haskell installation process is generally simple and quick. Keep reading to learn how to install Haskell on your computer.

Installing Haskell on macOS

If you have a macOS computer, you can install Haskell using the Homebrew package manager. To install Homebrew, open the terminal and enter the following command:

/bin/bash -c "$(curl -fsSL https://raw.githubusercontent.com/Homebrew/install/master/install.sh)"

Once Homebrew is installed, you can install GHC by entering the following command in the terminal:

brew install ghc

Next, you can install the GHCi interactive compiler by typing:

brew install ghc --with-interactive

Finally, to install Haskell Platform, enter the following command:

brew cask install haskell-platform

After the installation is completed, you can check that Haskell has been installed correctly by running the following commands in the terminal:

ghc --version

ghci

If everything has gone well, you should see the GHC compiler and GHCi interactive compiler versions running correctly in the console.

Installing Haskell on Linux

If you are using a Linux operating system, you can install Haskell using the package manager of your preferred Linux distribution. For instance, if you are using Ubuntu, you can install Haskell through the apt package manager by typing the following command in the terminal:

sudo apt-get update -y

sudo apt-get install -y haskell-platform

Once the installation is completed, you can verify that Haskell has been installed correctly by running the following commands in the terminal:

ghc --version

ghci

If everything has gone well, you should see the GHC compiler and GHCi interactive compiler versions running correctly in the console.

Installing Haskell on Windows

If you are using a Windows operating system, you can install Haskell using the GHC installation tool available on the official Haskell website (https://www.haskell.org/platform/). Download the installation file and run the installer following the on-screen instructions.

During the installation, make sure to select the option to install GHCi along with the GHC compiler in order to use the Haskell interactive interpreter. After completing the installation, you can check that Haskell has been installed correctly by opening the command prompt and typing the following commands:

ghc --version

ghci

If everything has gone well, you should see the GHC compiler and GHCi interactive compiler versions running correctly in the console.

Conclusion

In this article, we have explored how to install Haskell on your computer using different platforms. From macOS to Linux to Windows, there are various options available for installing Haskell and starting to develop projects with this powerful functional programming language.

Regardless of the platform you use, installing Haskell is generally a simple and quick process. With GHC, GHCi, and Haskell Platform at your disposal, you will be well-equipped to start exploring the capabilities of Haskell and creating innovative and efficient projects.

3. Basic Syntax of Haskell

The basic syntax of Haskell is a fundamental topic to understand in order to program in this functional language. Haskell is a pure and lazy programming language, which means that evaluations of expressions are only performed when necessary and no state changes are made.

The syntax of Haskell is based on a set of rules that define how to correctly write code so that the compiler can compile it correctly. These rules include defining functions, declaring variables, and handling conditional and recursive expressions.

To start writing code in Haskell, it is important to know the basics of the syntax. One distinctive feature of Haskell is strong static typing, which means that each expression and value has a well-defined type that cannot be changed once it has been defined.

A key concept in Haskell is the definition and application of functions. Functions in Haskell are defined using the keyword "fun" followed by the function name, parameters in parentheses, and the function body separated by an equal sign. For example, the following function in Haskell calculates the double of a number:

```Haskell
double :: Int -> Int
double x = x * 2
```

In this example, "double" is the function name, "Int" is the type of the input parameter, and "Int" is the output type of the function. The function body is "x * 2", which calculates the double of the input number.

Variable declaration in Haskell is similar to function definition. Variables are declared using the keyword "let" followed by the variable name, the assignment operator, and the value of the variable. For example, the following variable declaration in Haskell assigns the value 10 to the variable "x":

```Haskell

let x = 10

```

Conditional expressions in Haskell are defined using the keyword "if" followed by a condition, the comparison operator, and the result if the condition is true, and finally the comparison operator and the result if the condition is false. For example, the following conditional expression in Haskell returns the maximum of two numbers:

```Haskell
maxNum :: Int -> Int -> Int
maxNum a b = if a > b then a else b
```

In this example, "maxNum" is the function name, "Int -> Int -> Int" indicates that the function takes two Int parameters and returns an Int value. The function compares the two inputs "a" and "b" and returns the larger value.

Recursive expressions are common in Haskell as the language supports recursion natively. A recursive function is a function that calls itself during its execution. For example, the following function in Haskell calculates the factorial of a number using recursion:

```Haskell
factorial :: Int -> Int
```

```
factorial 0 = 1

factorial n = n * factorial (n - 1)
```

In this example, "factorial" is the function name that calculates the factorial of a number. The implementation of the function uses a base case for the number 0 and a recursive case that calculates the factorial of number "n" by multiplying it with the factorial of "n-1".

Another important feature of Haskell syntax is handling lists and tuples. Lists in Haskell are defined using square brackets and elements of the list are separated by commas. For example, the following list in Haskell contains three Int elements:

```Haskell
myList :: [Int]

myList = [1, 2, 3]
```

```

Tuples in Haskell are defined using parentheses and tuple elements are separated by commas. For example, the following tuple in Haskell contains two elements of type Int and String:

```Haskell

myTuple :: (Int, String)

myTuple = (1, "hello")

```

In addition to functions, variables, conditional expressions, recursive expressions, lists, and tuples, Haskell syntax includes many other features such as higher-order functions, anonymous functions, pattern matching expressions, and error handling. With a good understanding of the basic syntax of Haskell, it is possible to write efficient and intuitive
```

code that fully leverages the capabilities of this functional language.

4.Types of data in Haskell

Haskell is a functional programming language that uses a very sophisticated and powerful type system. Data types in Haskell are a fundamental part of the language and are one of the aspects that make it so powerful and flexible. In this article, we will explore the various data types available in Haskell and see how we can use them to write more robust and secure code.

Before we begin discussing data types in Haskell, it is important to understand what a data type is in general. A data type is a characteristic of a variable that defines the type of value it can assume. For example, a boolean data type can only assume two values: true or false. Data types help define how values can be used and how they can interact with each other.

In Haskell, data types are statically typed,

which means the type of every expression is known at compile time. This helps prevent many common type-related errors that can occur during program execution. Additionally, Haskell uses a very advanced type inference that allows the compiler to deduce the type of expressions even without the need to explicitly specify it.

Data types in Haskell can be divided into different categories based on the type of data they represent. Here are some of the main categories:

1. Primitive data types:

Haskell provides a series of primitive data types that represent the basic data types of the language. Some examples include:

- Int: represents integers

- Char: represents characters

- Bool: represents boolean values (true or false)

- Float: represents single-precision floating point numbers

- Double: represents double-precision floating point numbers

These data types are among the most common and are used to represent basic data in Haskell programs.

2. Complex data types:

In addition to primitive data types, Haskell allows the definition of complex data types, which are data types that can be composed of multiple data types. This allows for creating more complex and flexible data structures. Some examples of complex data types are:

- Tuple: an ordered set of values of different types. For example, a tuple (Int, Bool) represents a pair of an integer and a boolean.

- Lists: a sequence of values of the same type. For example, [Int] represents a list of integers.

- Data types: it is possible to define new data types using the keyword data. For example, data Tree a = Leaf a | Node (Tree a) (Tree a) defines a new tree data type that can contain values of type a in nodes or leaves.

3. Polymorphic data types:

In Haskell, it is possible to define polymorphic data types, which are data types that can contain values of different types. This makes the code more flexible and reusable. For example, the function head :: [a] -> a returns the first element of a list of type a, regardless of the data type contained in the list.

4. Algebraic data types:

Algebraic data types in Haskell allow the definition of complex data types using a combination of simpler data types. The two main types of algebraic data types are:

- Enumerated types: allow defining a finite set

of possible values that a variable can assume. For example, data Day = Monday | Tuesday | Wednesday | Thursday | Friday | Saturday | Sunday defines an enumerated type for the days of the week.

- Recursive data types: allow defining data types that refer to themselves. For example, a binary tree can be recursively defined as data Tree a = Leaf a | Node (Tree a) (Tree a).

In addition to these main categories, Haskell offers a wide range of predefined data types and the ability to define new data types flexibly and powerfully. By using data types in Haskell effectively, it is possible to write safer, more robust, and maintainable code. Data types in Haskell are a fundamental part of the language and play a key role in defining the data and operations that can be performed on them. With a wide range of data types available and the ability to define new ones flexibly, Haskell offers many possibilities for writing sophisticated and high-quality code. Learning to use data types effectively is essential to becoming an expert Haskell programmer and fully harnessing the potential of the language.

5. Haskell Functions

Haskell is a purely functional programming language that offers a wide range of features and tools for writing complex programs concisely and efficiently. Functions are a key element of Haskell and play a fundamental role in data processing, structure manipulation, and algorithm implementation. In this article, we will delve into Haskell functions, examining their main features, applications, and advanced techniques for their definition and usage.

Functions in Haskell are first-class objects, which means they can be treated like any other data in the language, such as numbers or strings. This allows passing functions as arguments to other functions, returning functions as the result of other functions, and defining nested functions within other functions. This flexibility allows for writing more modular, reusable, and readable code, making it easier to handle complexity and maintain code over time.

Functions in Haskell are defined through defining equations, which are mathematical expressions that associate an output value with an input value or a set of input values. Equations are defined based on cases, where each case represents a different input scenario and produces a different output result. Function definition in Haskell is based on the concept of pattern matching, which allows comparing input values with predefined patterns and associating them with corresponding output values.

An important aspect of functions in Haskell is their purity, meaning the absence of side effects. This means that functions in Haskell do not have unintended effects on the system state or variables external to the function itself. This promotes writing safer, more predictable, and easier to test code, as well as fully leveraging the mathematical and algebraic properties of functions to achieve greater correctness and modularity in the code.

Functions in Haskell are evaluated according to the lazy evaluation model, meaning input values are evaluated only when they are actually needed to calculate the function's output value. This avoids the calculation of unused intermediate values and efficiently handles computations on infinite or undefined-size data structures. Lazy evaluation also allows exploiting function composition properties to define more efficient algorithms and concisely express data transformations.

Functions in Haskell can be defined in various ways, including anonymous functions, higher-order functions, partial functions, and recursive functions. Anonymous functions, or lambda expressions, are nameless functions defined on-the-fly and used locally within other functions. Higher-order functions accept other functions as arguments or return other functions as results, allowing to implement common programming patterns like map, filter, and fold on data collections. Partial functions are functions defined with missing input values, which need to be provided later to obtain the complete output value. Recursive functions call themselves recursively to solve a larger problem by breaking it down into smaller problems.

Functions in Haskell support functional composition, which represents the ability to combine multiple functions together to create new, more complex functions. Functional composition allows for writing more modular and flexible code, reducing code duplication and facilitating managing dependencies between various parts of the program. For example, composing two functions f and g is represented as f . g x = f (g x), where function g is applied first and function f is applied subsequently to the result of g. Functional composition can be used to compose higher-order functions, recursive functions, anonymous functions, and any other type of function in Haskell.

Functions in Haskell can work with various data types, including numbers, lists, tuples, records, trees, and custom objects. Haskell provides a range of predefined data types and a static type system that ensures typical correctness of code at compile time, reducing the possibility of type errors during program execution. This allows writing more robust, less error-prone, and easily maintainable code over time. Additionally, Haskell supports defining algebraic data types, which allow combining basic types and data constructors to create new complex types and represent more complex data structures.

Functions in Haskell can be used to solve a wide range of problems, including data processing, manipulating complex structures, implementing search, sorting, and filtering algorithms, and designing interactive user interfaces. Haskell offers an expressive and concise syntax for defining functions, allowing for writing more compact and readable code compared to other programming languages. Furthermore, Haskell supports functions as first-class objects, meaning functions can be passed, returned, and manipulated flexibly and dynamically within the program.

1. Example of a function that calculates the double of a number:

```haskell
double :: Int -> Int
double x = x * 2
```

2. Example of a function that calculates the sum of numbers from 1 to n:

```haskell
```

```haskell
sumN :: Int -> Int
sumN n = sum [1..n]
```

3. Example of a function that checks if a number is even:

```haskell
isEven :: Int -> Bool
isEven x = x `mod` 2 == 0
```

4. Example of a function that returns the maximum of two numbers:

```haskell
maxNum :: Int -> Int -> Int
maxNum x y = if x > y then x else y
```

```

5. Example of a function that returns the length of a list:

```haskell
length :: [a] -> Int
length [] = 0
length (x:xs) = 1 + length xs
```

Functions in Haskell represent one of the foundational pillars of the language and enable writing more modular, flexible, efficient, and safe code. Haskell functions support a wide range of features and advanced techniques, including pattern matching, lazy evaluation, functional composition, static typing, and algebraic data types, allowing for elegantly and efficiently solving a wide range of problems. Haskell is widely used in
```

academic and industrial settings for developing high-level applications, distributed systems, and complex algorithms, thanks to its expressive power and mathematical robustness.

6. Haskell List Comprehension

The concept of list comprehension. This technique allows to create lists in a concise and readable way, making it easier to write efficient and easy-to-understand code.

List comprehensions in Haskell are very similar to those found in other programming languages such as Python, and allow to build lists by applying transformations to their elements or filtering them according to specific criteria. The basic syntax for defining a list comprehension is as follows:

```
[expression | element <- list, predicate]
```

Where "expression" is the transformation to apply to the elements of the list, "element" is a variable representing the elements of the starting list, "list" is the starting list on which to apply the transformations, and "predicate" is an optional condition that must be satisfied by the elements of the starting list.

For example, suppose we want to build a list of squares of numbers between 1 and 10. This operation can be easily achieved using list comprehension in Haskell:

```
squares = [x * x | x <- [1..10]]
```

In this case, the list comprehension creates a list of squares of numbers between 1 and 10, applying the transformation `x * x` to each element of the list `[1..10]`.

Another example of using list comprehension

is selecting elements that meet certain criteria. For example, suppose we want to select only the even numbers from the list `[1..10]`. This task can be easily accomplished using a predicate within the list comprehension:

```
evenNumbers = [x | x <- [1..10], even x]
```

In this case, the list comprehension selects only the elements from `[1..10]` that satisfy the predicate `even x`, meaning the even numbers.

List comprehensions can also be nested, allowing to combine multiple transformations and filters within a single expression. For example, suppose we want to build a list of tuples of numbers between 1 and 5, where the first element of the tuple is the number itself and the second element is its square. This operation can be achieved using a nested list comprehension:

```
tupleSquares = [(x, x * x) | x <- [1..5]]
```

In this case, the list comprehension creates a list of tuples `(x, x * x)` for each element in `[1..5]`. Each tuple contains the number itself as the first element and its square as the second element.

List comprehensions in Haskell are a powerful tool that allows to create lists quickly and concisely, simplifying the code writing and making it more readable. They are particularly useful for transforming and filtering lists efficiently, allowing to express complex concepts in just a few lines of code. Their intuitive syntax and versatility make them a fundamental tool for anyone programming in

Haskell.

7. Haskell Pattern Matching

Haskell is a very powerful functional language that offers a unique and powerful approach to pattern matching. Pattern matching is a technique used to extract information from a data structure in a concise and elegant way. In Haskell, pattern matching is tightly integrated into the language and is used in many different situations, such as function definitions, condition expressions, and assignment operations.

One of the most distinctive features of pattern matching in Haskell is its ability to handle complex data types transparently. For example, you can define functions that accept arguments of different types and use pattern matching to deal with the different cases separately. This allows you to write clearer and more maintainable code, avoiding the typical error handling problems that arise with the use of conditional statements and loops.

A common example of using pattern matching in Haskell is defining recursive functions that operate on lists. For example, let's take the function to calculate the length of a list:

```haskell
length' :: [a] -> Int
length' [] = 0
length' (_:xs) = 1 + length' xs
```

In this case, pattern matching is used to handle two cases: the empty list and the non-empty list. If the list is empty, the length is 0. Otherwise, it recurses on the tail of the list and adds 1 to the result. This example shows how pattern matching in Haskell allows you to write readable and concise code to manipulate complex data structures like lists.

Another common application of pattern matching in Haskell is handling user-defined data types through algebraic data types. These data types are composed of multiple constructors, each of which can have a different number of arguments. For example, we can define a data type to represent geometric shapes like circles and rectangles:

```haskell
data Shape = Circle Float | Rectangle Float Float
```

Using pattern matching, we can write functions that operate on Shape type data cleanly and concisely. For example, we can define a function to calculate the area of a Shape:

```haskell
```

```
area :: Shape -> Float
area (Circle r) = pi * r ^ 2
area (Rectangle w h) = w * h
```

In this case, pattern matching is used to distinguish between the two constructors of the Shape type and handle their arguments separately. This approach makes it easy to write code that handles different types of geometric shapes cleanly and maintainably.

In addition to function and data type definitions, pattern matching can also be used in conditional and assignment expressions. For example, we can use pattern matching to extract elements from a list elegantly:

```haskell
firstElement :: [a] -> Maybe a
```

```
firstElement [] = Nothing

firstElement (x:_) = Just x
```
```

In this case, pattern matching is used to extract the first element from the list. If the list is empty, we return Nothing. Otherwise, we return the first element as Just x. This approach is safer and more elegant than using functions like head that could throw an exception if the list is empty.

In conclusion, pattern matching is a powerful and flexible technique that plays a fundamental role in functional programming in Haskell. Thanks to its expressive syntax and integrated support in the language, pattern matching allows you to write clear, concise, and maintainable code to manipulate complex data structures and handle different cases elegantly. By using pattern matching, you can fully leverage the capabilities of Haskell and create high-quality code that is easy to
```

understand and maintain.

8. Haskell Recursion

Recursion is a fundamental concept in functional programming, and Haskell is a language that supports it in a very powerful and flexible way. In Haskell, recursion can be used to define functions that call themselves, allowing elegant and concise solutions to problems.

To better understand how recursion works in Haskell, let's see some practical examples. Let's start with a simple recursive function that calculates the factorial of a positive integer:

```haskell
factorial :: Int -> Int
factorial 0 = 1
factorial n = n * factorial (n - 1)
```

In this case, the `factorial` function has two base cases: when the argument is zero, the result is 1, otherwise it is calculated as the product of the argument and the factorial of the argument decremented by one. This is a classic example of a recursive function, calling itself on a smaller input until reaching the base case.

Another common example of recursion is the sum of numbers from 1 to n:

```haskell
sumTo :: Int -> Int
sumTo 0 = 0
sumTo n = n + sumTo (n - 1)
```

In this case as well, the `sumTo` function

recursively calls itself on a smaller input, eventually reaching the base case when the argument is zero.

An important aspect of recursion in Haskell is its readability and conciseness. Recursive functions can often be written in a very clear and elegant way, especially when dealing with problems that naturally lend themselves to a recursive solution.

Another interesting example is the `fibonacci` function, which calculates the nth Fibonacci number using recursion:

```haskell
fibonacci :: Int -> Int
fibonacci 0 = 0
fibonacci 1 = 1
fibonacci n = fibonacci (n-1) + fibonacci (n-2)
```

```

In this case, we have two base cases that return the first two Fibonacci numbers, and then we calculate the subsequent numbers by adding the two previous numbers. This is also an elegant recursive solution to a mathematical problem.

Another interesting feature of recursion in Haskell is the ability to define higher-order recursive functions, which take other functions as arguments. For example, we can define the `map` function using recursion:

```haskell
myMap :: (a -> b) -> [a] -> [b]
myMap _ [] = []
myMap f (x:xs) = f x : myMap f xs
```
```

In this case, the `myMap` function takes a function `f` and a list of elements `x` as arguments, and returns a new list where the function `f` has been applied to each element of the input list. This is another form of recursion that showcases the flexibility of the Haskell language in handling higher-order recursive functions.

Recursion is an important and powerful concept in Haskell, allowing for elegant and concise problem-solving. Recursive functions can be written clearly and readably, and Haskell provides the necessary tools to work efficiently with recursion, whether for simple functions like factorial and sum of numbers, or for more complex functions involving higher-order recursive functions.

9. Advanced data types in Haskell

One of the most commonly used advanced data types in Haskell is represented by lists. Lists are ordered sequences of elements of the same type, which can be of arbitrary length. For example, a list of integers could be defined in Haskell as follows:

```haskell
listInt :: [Int]

listInt = [1, 2, 3, 4]
```

Lists in Haskell are homogeneous, meaning that all elements within a list must be of the same type. However, it is possible to create lists of different types using data types such as tuples or nested lists. For example, a list of tuples of integers and strings could be defined as follows:

```haskell
listTuple :: [(Int, String)]
```

listTuple = [(1, "one"), (2, "two"), (3, "three")]
```

Another advanced data type in Haskell is represented by tuples. Tuples are ordered collections of a fixed number of elements of different types. For example, a tuple containing an integer and a string could be defined as follows:

```haskell

tuple :: (Int, String)

tuple = (42, "Hello, World!")
```

Tuples allow Haskell developers to create more complex and flexible data structures compared to lists, as they can contain a combination of different types within the same object.

Another advanced data type in Haskell is represented by records. Records are data
```

structures composed of different fields, each of which contains a value of a specific type. The fields of a record are generally accessible using their name. For example, a record representing a person could be defined as follows:

```haskell
data Person = Person {name :: String, age :: Int}
```

In this case, the Person record contains two fields: name of type String and age of type Int. An instance of the Person record can be created by specifying values for each field as follows:

```haskell
person :: Person
person = Person {name = "Alice", age = 30}
```

Once a record is created, its fields can be accessed using dot syntax. For example, to get the name of the person defined above, the following code can be used:

```haskell
personName :: String

personName = name person
```

In addition to lists, tuples, and records, Haskell offers a variety of advanced data types to handle more complex structures, such as trees, graphs, and monads. For example, algebraic data types are widely used in Haskell to represent structured data in a repeatable and recursive manner. An example of an algebraic data type in Haskell could be the following:

```haskell
data Tree a = Leaf a | Node (Tree a) a (Tree a)
```

In this case, a Tree can be a Leaf containing a value of type a or a Node containing a value of type a and two sub-trees of type Tree a. This representation allows for the creation and manipulation of trees of various shapes and sizes efficiently and safely.

Another advanced data type in Haskell is monads. Monads allow for the efficient handling of operations involving side effects, such as I/O, state, or exceptions. Monads enable writing cleaner and more maintainable code by separating application logic from actual operations. An example of a monad in Haskell is the Maybe monad, which handles the concept of optional values. The Maybe monad can be defined as follows:

```haskell
data Maybe a = Just a | Nothing
```

The Maybe monad contains two possible values: Just a representing a concrete value of type a or Nothing representing the absence of a value. This allows Haskell developers to safely handle cases where a value may not be present, avoiding runtime errors and improving edge case management.

Haskell offers a wide range of advanced data types that allow developers to write more robust, efficient, and secure code. From lists to tuples, records to monads, these data types enable efficient handling of a wide range of information within a program, allowing Haskell developers to focus on the application logic without worrying about the implementation details of data management. Thanks to these advanced data types, Haskell remains one of the most powerful and flexible functional programming languages available on the market.

10. Higher-order functions Recursive functions in Haskell

In Haskell, higher-order functions play a fundamental role in functional programming. Higher-order functions are functions that take other functions as arguments or return functions as results. This concept is at the core of functional programming and allows us to write more efficient and expressive code.

An example of a higher-order function in Haskell is the `map` function. The `map` function takes a function as an argument and a list, and applies the function to each element of the list, returning a new list with the results. For example, if we have a list of numbers and we want to double each number, we can use `map` like this:

```haskell
double :: Int -> Int
```

```
double x = x * 2

numbers = [1, 2, 3, 4]
doubledNumbers = map double numbers
```

In this example, the `double` function is a higher-order function because it is passed as an argument to the `map` function.

Another example of a higher-order function is the `filter` function. The `filter` function takes a predicate function and a list, and returns a list containing only the elements that satisfy the predicate. For example, if we want to filter out even numbers from a list of numbers, we can use `filter` like this:

```haskell
evenNumber :: Int -> Bool
```

```
evenNumber x = x `mod` 2 == 0


numbers = [1, 2, 3, 4]

evenNumbers = filter evenNumber numbers
```

In this case, the `evenNumber` function is a higher-order function as it is passed as an argument to the `filter` function.

Recursive functions are another important feature of functional programming, where a function calls itself within its body. Haskell supports recursion in various ways, including direct recursion and recursion through higher-order functions like `foldr` and `foldl`.

An example of a recursive function in Haskell is the `factorial` function, which calculates the factorial of a number. The recursive definition of the factorial is as follows:

```haskell
factorial :: Int -> Int
factorial 0 = 1
factorial n = n * factorial (n-1)
```

In this example, the `factorial` function is defined using direct recursion. If the parameter `n` is zero, the factorial is 1. Otherwise, the factorial of `n` is `n` multiplied by the factorial of `n-1`.

Another example of a recursive function is the `fibonacci` function, which calculates the Fibonacci number of a number. The recursive definition of the Fibonacci sequence is as follows:

```haskell
```

```
fibonacci :: Int -> Int

fibonacci 0 = 0

fibonacci 1 = 1

fibonacci n = fibonacci (n-1) + fibonacci (n-2)
```
```

In this example, the `fibonacci` function is defined using direct recursion. If the parameter `n` is zero, the Fibonacci number is 0. If it is one, the Fibonacci number is 1. Otherwise, the Fibonacci number of `n` is the sum of the Fibonacci numbers of `n-1` and `n-2`.

Recursion is not the only way to solve problems in Haskell. We can also use higher-order functions like `foldr` and `foldl` to solve recursive problems in a more elegant way.

For example, we can rewrite the `factorial` function using `foldr` like this:
```

```haskell
factorial :: Int -> Int
factorial n = foldr (*) 1 [1..n]
```

In this case, `foldr` combines the elements of the list `[1..n]` using the multiplication operator `(*)`. Additionally, we can implement the `fibonacci` function using `foldl` like this:

```haskell
fibonacci :: Int -> Int
fibonacci n = snd $ foldl (\(a, b) _ -> (b, a + b)) (0, 1) [0..n]
```

Here, `foldl` combines the elements of the list

`[0..n]` using a lambda function that updates the state `(a, b)` based on the previous values.

Higher-order functions and recursive functions are fundamental elements of functional programming in Haskell. By using these techniques, we can write more elegant and concise code, avoiding the need for loops and mutable variables. This approach allows us to create more readable, maintainable, and efficient programs.

11. Haskell Lambda Functions

Haskell is a functional programming language that offers many advanced features, including lambda functions. Lambda functions are anonymous functions that can be defined concisely and used directly in the code without the need to assign them a name. They can be used to create ad hoc functions quickly and efficiently. In Haskell, lambda functions are defined using the syntax `\ parameter -> expression`.

For example, consider a function that takes an integer and returns its square. We can define this lambda function in Haskell as follows:

```haskell
square = \x -> x * x
```

This lambda function takes an argument `x` and returns its square by multiplying `x` by itself. We can use this function in Haskell code without explicitly defining it with a name:

```haskell
main = do
  let result = square 5
  print result
```

In this case, we directly call the `square` function with the argument 5 and print the result, which will be 25.

Lambda functions can also take more than one parameter. For example, suppose we want to create a function that calculates the sum of two numbers. We can do this by defining a lambda function with two parameters as follows:

```haskell
sum = \x y -> x + y
```

This lambda function takes two arguments `x` and `y` and returns their sum. We can use this function in Haskell code as follows:

```haskell
main = do
  let result = sum 3 4
  print result
```

In this case, the `sum` function is called with the arguments 3 and 4 and returns 7, which is then printed to the screen.

Lambda functions can also be used as arguments to other functions. For example, suppose we have a function that applies a specific transformation to all elements of a list. We can use a lambda function to define this transformation concisely. Suppose we want to double each element of a list of integers. We can do this using the `map` function along with a lambda function:

```haskell
doubleList = map (\x -> x * 2)
```

This lambda function takes an argument `x` and returns its double by multiplying `x` by 2. The `map` function applies this transformation to all elements of the list. We can use this function in Haskell code like this:

```haskell
```

```
main = do
  let numbers = [1, 2, 3, 4, 5]
  let doubledNumbers = doubleList numbers
  print doubledNumbers
```

In this case, the `doubleList` function is applied to the list of numbers `[1, 2, 3, 4, 5]`, and the numbers are doubled. The result will be a new list `[2, 4, 6, 8, 10]`.

Lambda functions can be useful for creating simple and ad hoc functions directly in the code without the need to explicitly define them with a name. They can make the code more concise and readable, especially when it comes to quick and specific transformations.

In conclusion, lambda functions are a powerful feature of Haskell that allows you to define anonymous functions concisely and directly. They can be used to create ad hoc functions, pass them as arguments to other functions, and make the code clearer and more readable. With the syntax `\ parameter -> expression`, it is easy to create and use lambda functions in Haskell to solve a variety of problems efficiently and elegantly.

12. Monads and Functional Programming

Functional programming is a programming paradigm based on the application of mathematical functions to solve problems instead of changing the state of variables. Haskell is a functional programming language that is based on Church's algebra.

One of the main features of Haskell is the concept of monads. Monads are a mathematical structure that allows for efficient handling of side effects within a functional program. Monads in Haskell were first introduced by Philip Wadler and Joseph Stoy in 1992 and revolutionized the way developers can manage side effects in their programs.

Monads in Haskell are an abstract data structure that contains a value and the operations that can be performed on that value. A monad is defined by two functions:

`return` and `bind`. The `return` function takes a value and wraps it in the monad, while the `bind` function takes a monad and a function that takes a value and returns another monad.

A simple example of a monad is the Identity monad. This monad takes a value and returns it without any modification. Here is how it could be defined in Haskell:

```haskell
newtype Identity a = Identity { runIdentity :: a }

instance Monad Identity where
  return a = Identity a
  m >>= k = k (runIdentity m)
```

The Identity monad does not introduce any

side effects to our program, but it is useful for understanding the basic concepts of how monads work in Haskell. Monads are primarily used to handle operations involving side effects such as I/O, exception throwing, and error handling.

Monads are widely used in Haskell to combine functions that produce side effects in a composable and safe manner. A common example of using monads is string parsing. Haskell provides the `Parsec` library, which uses monads to combine parsers of different types safely and efficiently.

Another example of using monads in Haskell is handling I/O. Haskell is a purely functional language, which means it does not allow impure I/O that could have unpredictable side effects on the program. To handle I/O safely in Haskell, you can use the `IO` monad.

The `IO` monad in Haskell provides a secure

interface for impure I/O. For example, if we want to print a message to the screen, we can do so using the `putStrLn` function, which returns a value of type `IO ()`, indicating that a side effect is involved.

```haskell
main :: IO ()
main = do
  putStrLn "Hello, world!"
```

In this example, the `putStrLn` function creates an I/O action of type `IO ()` that is combined using the `IO` monad. Monads allow for combining I/O actions in a composable and safe manner, ensuring that the order of execution of actions is respected.

Monads in Haskell offer an elegant way to handle side effects within functional programs. Monads provide a convenient interface for combining functions and managing operations involving side effects in a composable and safe manner.

Monads are a fundamental part of Haskell's functional programming and play a key role in managing side effects within programs. Using monads in Haskell allows for writing cleaner, composable, and safer code, enabling developers to efficiently and readably manage side effects.

13. Examples of writing Hello World in Haskell

To write a simple "Hello World" program in Haskell, we can use the simple function "putStrLn" which prints a string to the console.

Here is the code for the "Hello World" program in Haskell:

```haskell
main :: IO ()
main = putStrLn "Hello World"
```

In this example, we have defined the function "main" which is the entry point of our program. The function signature indicates that it will return a value of type IO (), which is the type for all input/output operations in Haskell. The body of the function is simply a call to the "putStrLn" function with the argument "Hello World", which is the string we want to print to the console.

To execute the "Hello World" program in Haskell, we need to save it in a file with the ".hs" extension, for example "hello.hs", and then compile and run the file using the GHC (Glasgow Haskell Compiler) compiler. Here is how we can do it:

1. Create a new file called "hello.hs" and paste the Haskell code for the "Hello World" program inside the file.

2. Open a terminal and navigate to the directory where the "hello.hs" file is located.

3. Compile the file using the GHC compiler with the following command:

```

ghc -o hello hello.hs

```

This command will compile the "hello.hs" file and create an executable file called "hello".

4. Run the executable file "hello" with the following command:

```

./hello

```

This command will run the program and print "Hello World" to the console.

Here is an example of the output we would see in the console after running the "Hello World" program in Haskell:

```
```

Hello World

```


```

In this way, we have successfully written and executed a simple "Hello World" program in Haskell, leveraging the strong static typing and simplicity of functional programming. Haskell is a powerful and expressive language that allows for writing concise and elegant code, even for programs as simple as this one.

14. Lists in Haskell

In Haskell, lists are one of the fundamental data structures and are widely used to store a sequence of elements of the same type. Lists are defined recursively and can be either empty or formed by an element (the head of the list) followed by another list (the tail of the list). For example, the list `[1,2,3]` is formed by the element `1` followed by the list `[2,3]`, which in turn is formed by `2` followed by `[3]`, which then is a list formed by `3` followed by the empty list `[]`.

Lists in Haskell can contain elements of any type, but all elements within the same list must have the same type. For example, the list `[1, "hello", True]` is not valid in Haskell because it contains elements of different types.

Here are some examples of how lists can be defined and manipulated in Haskell:

1. List Definition:

Lists can be defined in Haskell in various ways. Here are some examples:

- Empty list: `[]`
- List of integers: `[1,2,3,4,5]`
- List of characters: `['a','b','c','d','e']`
- List of strings: `["hello", "world"]`

2. Basic List Operations:

Haskell provides predefined functions to manipulate lists. Here are some basic operations:

- List concatenation:

```haskell
list1 = [1,2,3]
```

```haskell
list2 = [4,5,6]

concatenated = list1 ++ list2

-- The result will be [1,2,3,4,5,6]
```

- Adding elements at the end of the list:

```haskell
list = [1,2,3]

added = list ++ [4]

-- The result will be [1,2,3,4]
```

- Taking the first element of the list (the head):

```haskell
list = [1,2,3]

headElement = head list
```

-- The result will be 1
```

- Taking all elements except the first one (the tail):

```haskell
list = [1,2,3]

tailElements = tail list

-- The result will be [2,3]
```

- Getting the length of the list:

```haskell
list = [1,2,3,4,5]

length = length list

-- The result will be 5
```
```

3. Pattern Matching on Lists:

One of the most powerful features of Haskell is the ability to perform pattern matching on lists. This allows you to write functions that behave differently depending on the pattern of the list passed as an argument. Here is an example of a function that calculates the sum of elements in a list using pattern matching:

```haskell
sumList :: [Int] -> Int
sumList [] = 0
sumList (x:xs) = x + sumList xs
```

In the code above, the `sumList` function is defined recursively, with the base case handling the empty list and the recursive case calling itself to calculate the sum of the remaining elements.

Lists are a fundamental part of functional

programming in Haskell and are widely used to represent sequences of elements of the same type. Lists can be easily manipulated using the predefined functions provided by Haskell and are often the ideal choice for storing structured data flexibly and dynamically.

15. Tuple in Haskell

In Haskell, a tuple is a data structure that allows grouping a fixed number of values of different types within a single entity. Tuples are a very flexible data type and can be used to represent various concepts, such as coordinates, contact information, input data for functions, etc.

The syntax for defining a tuple in Haskell is very simple, using parentheses "(" to open the tuple, and separating the values with a comma ",". For example, a tuple that contains two values, one of type Int and one of type Char, can be defined as follows:

```haskell
tuple1 :: (Int, Char)
tuple1 = (42, 'a')
```

In this case, the tuple `tuple1` contains two values, `42` of type Int and `'a'` of type Char. It is important to note that the type of the tuple is defined within parentheses after the double colon `::`, in this case `(Int, Char)`.

Tuples in Haskell can contain an arbitrary number of values, so it is possible to have tuples with 3, 4, 5 values, and so on. For example:

```haskell
tuple2 :: (Int, Char, String)
tuple2 = (10, 'b', "Hello")
```

In this case, the tuple `tuple2` contains three values of different types: `10` of type Int, `'b'` of type Char, and `"Hello"` of type String.

Tuples in Haskell also allow nesting tuples within other tuples, creating complex and hierarchical data structures. For example:

```haskell
tuple3 :: ((Int, Char), (Float, Bool))
tuple3 = ((42, 'c'), (3.14, False))
```

In this case, the tuple `tuple3` contains two nested tuples, the first with an Int and a Char, and the second with a Float and a Bool.

To access individual elements of a tuple in Haskell, you can use the syntax `(fst tuple)` to get the first element and `(snd tuple)` to get the second element. For example:

```haskell
```

```haskell
x :: Int
x = fst tuple1 -- will return 42


y :: Char
y = snd tuple1 -- will return 'a'
```

It is important to note that the use of `fst` and `snd` is limited to tuples with two elements. For tuples with more elements, you can use pattern matching syntax to extract individual values. For example:

```haskell
f :: (Int, Char, Float) -> Int
f (x, _, _) = x
```

In this case, the function `f` takes a tuple with

three elements and returns the first element of the tuple.

Tuples in Haskell are commonly used to return multiple values as the output of a function, for example:

```haskell
sumAndProduct :: Int -> Int -> (Int, Int)
sumAndProduct x y = (x + y, x * y)
```

In this case, the function `sumAndProduct` takes two Int values as input and returns a tuple containing the sum and product of these two values.

Tuples in Haskell are a very important and flexible concept for managing and manipulating data of different types. Their simple syntax and the ability to nest tuples make them very useful in many situations, both for data representation and for handling function outputs.

16. Typeclasses in Haskell

In Haskell, typeclasses are a fundamental concept that allows defining common behaviors for different types of data. Typeclasses are similar to interfaces in object-oriented languages, but they are more powerful as they allow defining polymorphic functions that can be applied to different types of data.

A typeclass is defined using the keyword "class", followed by the name of the typeclass and the names of the type parameters separated by commas. For example, the following definition of the "Eq" typeclass represents a class of types where values can be compared for equality:

```
class Eq a where
    (==) :: a -> a -> Bool
```

```
(/=) :: a -> a -> Bool
```

In this case, the "Eq" typeclass requires a data type to be an instance of Eq if it is possible to define comparison operations for equality and inequality. For example, we can define an instance of the "Eq" typeclass for the Bool data type like this:

```
instance Eq Bool where
  True == True = True
  False == False = True
  _ == _ = False
```

In this case, we are defining that Bool values can be compared for equality and that two values are equal only if both are True or False.

Typeclasses can be used to define common behaviors for different types of data without resorting to ad-hoc programming. For example, the "Ord" typeclass is used to define the ordering of values in Haskell:

```
class Eq a => Ord a where
  compare :: a -> a -> Ordering
  (<) :: a -> a -> Bool
  (<=) :: a -> a -> Bool
  (>) :: a -> a -> Bool
  (>=) :: a -> a -> Bool
```

In this case, the "Ord" typeclass extends the "Eq" typeclass and requires a data type to be an instance of "Ord" if it is possible to compare values for ordering. For example, we can define an instance of the "Ord" typeclass for the Int data type like this:

```
instance Ord Int where
  compare x y
    | x < y = LT
    | x == y = EQ
    | otherwise = GT
```

In this case, we are defining that Int values can be compared for ordering based on the natural order of integers.

Typeclasses are a powerful functional programming tool that allows defining common behaviors for different types of data in an elegant and flexible way. They can be used to implement advanced features such as data serialization, input validation, and error handling in a modular and extensible manner. Typeclasses are a key concept in Haskell and are widely used in functional programming to ensure code correctness and modularity.

17. Monads in Haskell

Monads provide an elegant way to solve the problem of imperative programming within a functional language, allowing to handle operations like input/output, exception handling, and more.

A monad in Haskell is an algebraic structure that defines two fundamental operations: `return` and `bind`, which obey certain functionality laws. The `return` function takes a value and encapsulates it in the monad, while the `bind` function plays a key role in implementing the sequential concatenation of monadic actions.

A classic example of a monad in Haskell is the `Maybe` monad, which handles optional values. The definition of `Maybe` as a monad in Haskell is as follows:

```haskell
instance Monad Maybe where
    return x = Just x
    Nothing >>= f = Nothing
    (Just x) >>= f = f x
```

In this case, `return` takes a value and encapsulates it in `Just`, while `bind` applies the function `f` to the encapsulated value only if it is `Just`.

Another common example of a monad is the `IO` monad, used to handle input/output operations. One of the main features of the `IO` monad is that monadic actions are sequential and deterministic, ensuring that input/output operations are carried out in the correct order.

Here is an example of how you can combine IO monadic actions using Haskell's do notation:

```haskell
main :: IO ()
main = do
    putStrLn "Enter a number:"
    number <- getLine
    let double = (read number) * 2
    putStrLn ("The double of the entered number is: " ++ show double)
```

In this example, the `main` function executes a sequence of IO monadic actions, including output of a message, reading input from the keyboard, and printing the double of the entered number.

Another very useful example of a monad in Haskell is the `List` monad, which handles nondeterministic values. The definition of

`List` as a monad in Haskell is as follows:

```haskell
instance Monad [] where
    return x = [x]
    xs >>= f = concat (map f xs)
```

In this case, `return` takes a value and turns it into a list with a single element, while `bind` applies the function `f` to each element of the list and concatenates the results.

An example of how you can combine list monadic actions using Haskell's do notation is as follows:

```haskell
main :: IO ()
```

```haskell
main = do
    let numbers = [1, 2, 3]
    let doubles = do
        x <- numbers
        return (x * 2)
    putStrLn ("The double numbers are: " ++ show doubles)
```

In this example, the `main` function creates a list of numbers and applies the `(* 2)` function to each number, returning a list of the doubled numbers.

Lastly, another interesting example of a monad in Haskell is the `State` monad, used to handle the internal state of an application. The definition of `State` as a monad in Haskell is as follows:

```haskell
newtype State s a = State { runState :: s -> (a, s) }

instance Monad (State s) where
    return x = State (\s -> (x, s))
    (State f) >>= g = State (\s -> let (a, s') = f s
                                   in runState (g a) s')
```

In this case, `return` returns a new state with the element `x`, while `bind` applies the function `g` to the state and the value of the application of the function `f`.

An example of how you can combine state monadic actions using Haskell's do notation is as follows:

```haskell
```

```haskell
import Control.Monad.State

type StateExample = State Int Int

incrementState :: StateExample
incrementState = do
   state <- get
   put (state + 1)
   return state

main :: IO ()
main = do
   let (result, newState) = runState incrementState 0
   putStrLn ("The new state is: " ++ show newState)
```

18. Functors in Haskell

Functors are a fundamental part of functional programming, especially in the Haskell programming language. Functors are an abstract concept that allows mapping a function over a data type. In Haskell, functors are implemented through the `Functor` type class, which contains a single `fmap` method.

A functor in Haskell is a structure that represents a data type that can be mapped with a function. This means that a functor allows applying a function to each element within the data structure and returning a new structure with the results of the function applied to each element.

For example, consider the list as a functor in Haskell. The list is a data type that can contain zero or more elements of the same type. We can apply a function to each element of the list using the `map` operator. For instance, if we have a list of integers `[1, 2, 3]` and we want to multiply each element by 2, we can do so like this:

```haskell
list = [1, 2, 3]
result = map (*2) list
-- result will be [2, 4, 6]
```

In this example, the `map` function mapped the `(*2)` function to each element of the list, resulting in `[2, 4, 6]`.

The concept of functors can be generalized to any data type that can be mapped with a function. For example, we can define a new data type like a binary tree and implement a functor instance for this data type.

```haskell
data Tree a = Node a (Tree a) (Tree a) | Leaf
  deriving (Show)


instance Functor Tree where
  fmap f Leaf = Leaf
  fmap f (Node x left right) = Node (f x) (fmap f left) (fmap f right)


tree = Node 1 (Node 2 Leaf Leaf) (Node 3 Leaf Leaf)

result = fmap (*2) tree

-- result will be Node 2 (Node 4 Leaf Leaf) (Node 6 Leaf Leaf)
```

In this example, we defined a new data type `Tree` that can represent a binary tree with nodes and leaves. We then implemented a functor instance for the tree, defining how the `fmap` function should map a function over each node of the tree. In our example, we mapped the `(*2)` function over each node of the tree, resulting in a new tree with the results of the function applied to each node.

Functors are very useful in functional programming as they provide an elegant and general way to apply a function to a data type transparently. They can be used to solve various programming problems efficiently and concisely.

Additionally, functors in Haskell can be combined with other concepts like monads and applicatives to create more complex data structures and to handle side effects safely and concisely.

Functors are a fundamental part of functional programming in Haskell and provide a powerful way to manipulate data in a general and transparent manner. They are an essential tool for any programmer who wants to write clean, efficient, and safe code.

19. Applications in Haskell

Haskell is a functional programming language known for its strong static typing and elegant and concise syntax. It is widely used in theoretical computer science and scientific research, but developers also appreciate it for its ability to efficiently handle complex and parallelized computations.

One of the main advantages of Haskell is its rich ecosystem of libraries and frameworks that allow developers to create sophisticated and scalable applications. In particular, there are numerous applications in Haskell used in various sectors such as machine learning, data analysis, web development, and more. In this article, we will explore some examples of applications in Haskell and see how they can be used to solve different computational challenges.

One of the most well-known applications in

Haskell is Pandoc, a document converter that supports a wide range of formats including Markdown, HTML, PDF, LaTeX, and many others. Pandoc enables users to quickly and easily convert documents from one format to another while preserving the formatting and structure of the text. For example, if a user wants to convert a Markdown file to a PDF document, they can use Pandoc to perform this conversion in a few simple steps:

```
pandoc -s input.md -o output.pdf
```

In this case, the pandoc command instructs the software to convert the input.md file (containing Markdown text) to the output.pdf file (which will contain the converted PDF document). Pandoc is highly flexible and customizable, allowing users to specify additional options to control the formatting and structure of the output document.

Another example of an application in Haskell is QuickCheck, a framework for automatically testing the properties of functions and algorithms. QuickCheck allows developers to specify rules and invariants that must be satisfied by a particular function or algorithm, and it automatically generates random test data to verify if these properties are met. For instance, if a programmer wants to verify that a sorting function returns a sorted list, they can use QuickCheck to create automated tests in a few simple steps:

```haskell
import Test.QuickCheck

prop_ordered :: [Int] -> Bool
prop_ordered xs = isOrdered (sort xs)
  where isOrdered (x:y:ys) = x <= y && isOrdered (y:ys)
```

```
isOrdered _ = True


main :: IO ()

main = quickCheck prop_ordered
```
```

In this case, the program defines a property prop_ordered that specifies that a sorted list should return True when passed to the isOrdered function. Subsequently, the main function uses quickCheck to automatically test this property using randomly generated test data. QuickCheck is particularly useful for identifying hidden errors and vulnerabilities in programs, improving software quality and reliability.

Another popular application in Haskell is Hoogle, a search engine for libraries and modules available in the language. Hoogle allows developers to search for functions, data types, and other useful resources using
```

keywords and type signatures, making it easier to discover and use external libraries. For example, if a programmer is looking for a function to calculate the square root of a number in Haskell, they can use Hoogle to quickly find the corresponding function and understand how to use it in their code:

```haskell
sqrt :: Floating a => a -> a
```

In this case, a search on Hoogle would return the sqrt function, which calculates the square root of a Floating type number. By using Hoogle, developers can save time and effort in finding relevant libraries and modules, allowing them to focus on writing code more efficiently.

Lastly, a widely used application in Haskell is Yesod, a framework for developing scalable and high-performance web applications. Yesod provides a static template system, declarative routing, advanced security, and data persistence support, enabling developers to create dynamic and complex websites quickly and efficiently. For example, if a team of developers wants to create a web application for managing an online store, they can use Yesod to handle user interface, user authentication, image uploading, and much more:

```haskell
{-# LANGUAGE OverloadedStrings, QuasiQuotes, TemplateHaskell, TypeFamilies #-}

import Yesod

data App = App
```

```
mkYesod "App" [parseRoutes|
/ HomeR GET
/products ProductsR GET POST
/product/#Int ProductR GET
|]


instance Yesod App


getHomeR :: Handler Html
getHomeR = defaultLayout [whamlet|
Welcome to our online store!|]


getProductsR :: Handler Html
getProductsR = defaultLayout [whamlet|
Displaying list of products|]


postProductsR :: Handler Html
postProductsR = defaultLayout [whamlet|
```

```
Adding new product to store|]

getProductR :: Int -> Handler Html

getProductR productId = defaultLayout [whamlet|Displaying product with ID #{productId}|]


main :: IO ()

main = warp 3000 App
```
```

In this example, the program defines a Yesod application that handles four main routes for the home page, product display, adding new products, and displaying a single product. Yesod uses a type-based approach to ensure code correctness and security, allowing developers to create reliable and robust web applications.
```

Applications in Haskell offer numerous tools and resources that enable developers to tackle complex challenges and create high-quality software efficiently. Thanks to its static typing, elegant syntax, and rich ecosystem of libraries and frameworks, Haskell has established itself as one of the preferred choices for functional programming and scientific research. We hope this article has been helpful in understanding the potential and possibilities offered by applications in Haskell and inspiring new ideas and projects in the field of functional programming.

20. Error handling in Haskell

Error handling in Haskell is a crucial aspect of functional programming, as the language does not support exceptions like other imperative languages. In Haskell, errors are mainly handled through the `Either` data type, which represents a value of type `Either a b`, where `a` is the type of the error and `b` is the type of the correct value.

An example of error handling in Haskell could be the `safeDivide` function, which calculates the division between two numbers, handling the error of division by zero:

```haskell
safeDivide :: Double -> Double -> Either String Double
safeDivide _ 0 = Left "Division by zero"
safeDivide x y = Right (x / y)
```

```

In this case, if the second argument is zero, the function will return `Left "Division by zero"`, otherwise it will return `Right (x / y)`.

A common way to handle errors in Haskell is to use the `Either` monad along with the `either` function to handle the results. For example, we can write a `divideAndLog` function that calculates the division between two numbers and logs the errors:

```haskell
divideAndLog :: Double -> Double -> IO ()
divideAndLog x y = either
  putStrLn
  print
  (safeDivide x y)
```
```

In this case, if the division is successful, the result will be printed with `print`, otherwise the error will be printed with `putStrLn`.

Another common technique to handle errors in Haskell is to use the `ExceptT` library along with the `runExceptT` function, which makes error handling within a transformer monad easier. For example, we can write a `divideAndLog'` function that calculates the division between two numbers and logs the errors using `ExceptT`:

```haskell
import Control.Monad.Trans.Except

divideAndLog' :: Double -> Double -> IO ()
divideAndLog' x y = do
  result <- runExceptT (ExceptT (return (safeDivide x y)))
```

        either putStrLn print result
```

In this case, the `runExceptT` function is used to extract the value from `ExceptT` and return a value of type `IO (Either String Double)`, which is then handled with `either`.

In Haskell, it is also possible to define custom data types to handle errors more specifically. For example, we can define a `DivideError` data type to handle division errors:

```haskell
data DivideError = DivideByZero | InvalidInput String

safeDivide' :: Double -> Double -> Either DivideError Double
safeDivide' _ 0 = Left DivideByZero

```haskell
safeDivide' x y | y < 0 = Left (InvalidInput "Negative divisor")
                | otherwise = Right (x / y)
```

In this case, the `safeDivide'` function will return `Left DivideByZero` if the divisor is zero and `Left (InvalidInput "Negative divisor")` if the divisor is negative.

Finally, the `throw` function from the `Control.Monad.Trans.Except` package can be used to throw custom exceptions within an `ExceptT` transformer monad. For example, we can write a `divideAndLog'` function that handles custom division errors:

```haskell
divideAndLog'' :: Double -> Double -> IO ()
divideAndLog'' x y = do
```

```
  result <- runExceptT (do
    when (y < 0) (throw (InvalidInput "Negative divisor"))
    ExceptT (return (safeDivide' x y)))
  either (\err -> putStrLn ("Error: " ++ show err)) print result
```

In this case, the `throw` function is used to throw a custom error within `ExceptT`, which is then handled with `either`.

In conclusion, error handling in Haskell is a fundamental aspect of functional programming, and it can be done through the use of `Either`, the `Either` monad, the `ExceptT` library, custom data types, and custom exceptions. These tools allow for robust and flexible error handling within a Haskell program.

21. Inheritance in Haskell

In Haskell, inheritance is implemented through the concept of type classes and class instances. Type classes define a set of operations that must be implemented by a specific data type, while class instances connect a data type to a specific implementation of these operations.

To define a type class in Haskell, you use the `class` keyword followed by the class name and its type parameters. For example, we can define a type class called `Shape` that represents all geometric shapes:

```haskell
class Shape a where
  area :: a -> Double
  perimeter :: a -> Double
```

In the code above, the `Shape` class has two methods, `area` and `perimeter`, that must be implemented by every class instance. Both methods take a value of type `a` and return a `Double`.

To create a class instance, you use the `instance` keyword followed by the class name and the data type for which you are creating the instance. For example, we can create a class instance for the `Circle` data type representing a circle:

```haskell
data Circle = Circle Double

instance Shape Circle where
  area (Circle r) = pi * r * r
  perimeter (Circle r) = 2 * pi * r
```

```

In the code above, we are creating a class instance for the `Circle` data type. We implement the `area` and `perimeter` methods for the `Circle` type using the corresponding mathematical formula for a circle.

Now we can use the `area` and `perimeter` methods with values of type `Circle` as follows:

```haskell
myCircle = Circle 5
circleArea = area myCircle
circlePerimeter = perimeter myCircle
```

In this example, we create a circle with a radius of 5 and calculate its area and perimeter
```

using the methods defined in the `Shape` class.

Another interesting feature of inheritance in Haskell is the ability to define type classes with class constraints. This means that a type class can require its type parameters to satisfy certain other type classes. For example, we can define a type class called `Playable` that requires its type parameters to implement the `Show` type class:

```haskell
class Show a => Playable a where
  play :: a -> IO ()
```

In the code above, we are defining a type class `Playable` that requires its type parameters to satisfy the `Show` type class. This means that every class instance for `Playable` must also be a class instance for `Show`.

We can then create a class instance for a new data type called `Song` representing a song and satisfying the `Show` class constraint:

```haskell
data Song = Song String

instance Show Song where
  show (Song title) = "Song: " ++ title

instance Playable Song where
  play (Song title) = putStrLn ("Now playing: " ++ title)
```

In the code above, we are creating a class instance for the `Song` data type that has a `show` method defined for the `Show` class and a `play` method defined for the `Playable` class.

Now we can use the `play` method with values of type `Song` as follows:

```haskell
mySong = Song "Imagine"
play mySong
```

In this example, we create a song with the title "Imagine" and play it using the `play` method defined for the `Playable` class.

In summary, inheritance in Haskell is implemented through type classes and class instances. Type classes define a set of operations that must be implemented by a specific data type, while class instances connect a data type to a specific implementation of these operations. By using class constraints, you can define more complex requirements for type classes and class instances.

22. Lazy evaluation

Lazy evaluation is a key concept in functional programming, especially in the Haskell language. It is an evaluation strategy that delays the calculation of an expression until it is strictly necessary, thus avoiding unnecessary or expensive operations.

In Haskell, expressions are evaluated only when their value is actually required, which can lead to greater efficiency and clearer and more concise code writing. For example, consider the following function:

```haskell
f x = x * 2
```

If we call this function with a specific value, for example `f 3`, the evaluation will be immediate and the result will be `6`. However, if we pass this function as an argument to another function, such as:

```haskell
g = map f [1,2,3]
```

The `map` function applies a function to each element of a list, but in this case the evaluation of `f` is postponed until it is strictly necessary. This means that the result will be a list `[2,4,6]`, without the need to explicitly evaluate `f` for each element.

Another example of lazy evaluation is with the `take` operator which takes a certain number of elements from a list. For example, we can create an infinite list of positive integers and take only the first 5 elements:

```haskell
naturals = [1..]
firstFive = take 5 naturals
```

In this case, the list `naturals` is defined as all positive integers starting from 1, but thanks to lazy evaluation, the evaluation automatically stops after taking the first 5 elements.

Lazy evaluation is particularly useful when working with potentially infinite data structures, as it allows to avoid unnecessary calculations and optimize the program's performance. For example, we can define a list of even numbers:

```haskell
evenNumbers = filter even [1..]
```

In this case, the `evenNumbers` list is defined as all even integers, but the evaluation is postponed until it is strictly necessary. If we want to only take the first 10 even numbers from the list, we can write:

```haskell
firstTenEven = take 10 evenNumbers
```

Thanks to lazy evaluation, the calculation is only done for the first 10 elements of the list, avoiding unnecessary operations for the subsequent elements.

Furthermore, lazy evaluation allows for writing cleaner and clearer code, as it is possible to define composed functions without explicitly managing the evaluation order of expressions. For example, consider the following function that calculates the sum of squares of even numbers between 1 and a certain limit:

```haskell
sumOfSquareEvenNumbers limit = sum (map (^2) (filter even [1..limit]))
```

In this case, the evaluation of the `map`, `filter`, and `sum` functions is postponed until it is strictly necessary, allowing to write the code in a simpler and more readable way.

Lazy evaluation is a fundamental concept in functional programming, especially in the Haskell language, as it allows to optimize the program's performance by avoiding unnecessary calculations and simplifying code writing. Through this strategy of delayed evaluation, it is possible to work with potentially infinite data structures and define composite functions more efficiently and clearly.

Lazy evaluation is a key feature of Haskell that distinguishes it from many other programming languages. In Haskell, expressions are not evaluated until it is strictly necessary to do so. This behavior can lead to significant advantages in terms of efficiency and code simplicity.

A simple example of laziness in Haskell is given by the `listLength` function that calculates the length of a list recursively:

```haskell
listLength :: [a] -> Int
listLength [] = 0
listLength (_:xs) = 1 + listLength xs
```

Thanks to Haskell's laziness, only the first element of the list is evaluated at each recursive call, allowing the function to operate on infinite lists without exhausting memory.

Another example of laziness is given by the `infiniteList` function that generates an infinite list of integers:

```haskell
infiniteList :: [Int]
infiniteList = [1..]
```

This list is never fully generated in memory, but is evaluated only when strictly necessary. For example, we can use the `take` function to extract only the first ten elements of the infinite list:

```haskell
take 10 infiniteList
```

This calculates only the first ten elements of the infinite list without having to calculate the entire list.

Laziness in Haskell also allows for writing cleaner and more concise code, avoiding the need to evaluate unnecessary expressions. For example, we can define a `calculateSquare` function that calculates the square of a number only if it is greater than 10:

```haskell
calculateSquare :: Int -> Int
calculateSquare x
    | result > 10 = result
```

```
    | otherwise = 0
    where result = x * x
```

In this case, the variable `result` is evaluated only when necessary to return the function's result, avoiding evaluating the `x * x` expression if the result is less than 10.

Lastly, laziness in Haskell allows for defining more efficient data structures and algorithms thanks to the delayed evaluation of expressions. For example, we can implement a `maximum'` function that calculates the maximum value of a list without evaluating each individual element of the list:

```haskell
maximum' :: (Ord a) => [a] -> a
maximum' [] = error "Empty list"
```

```
maximum' (x:xs) = max x (maximum' xs)
```
```

In this case, the `max` function is evaluated only when necessary, reducing the number of actual evaluations and improving the overall code performance.

Laziness in Haskell is a fundamental feature that allows for writing more efficient, clean, and concise code. Through the delayed evaluation of expressions, Haskell can handle infinite lists, define more efficient algorithms, and avoid evaluating unnecessary expressions. Laziness is one of the reasons why Haskell is so powerful and flexible as a functional programming language.
```

23. Performance and Optimization in Haskell

Like any other programming language, Haskell can have weaknesses in terms of performance and optimization. In this text, we will delve into the main techniques to improve the performance of applications written in Haskell and to optimize the code efficiently.

One of the most important techniques to improve the performance of Haskell applications is the use of lazy evaluation functions. Haskell is a purely functional language that adopts a lazy evaluation strategy known as "call by need". This means that expressions are not evaluated until they are actually needed. This mechanism can lead to more efficient use of resources and greater parallelization of operations. For example, consider the following function that calculates the sum of the first n integers:

```
sumInts :: Int -> Int
sumInts n = sum [1..n]
```

In this case, the `sum` function is evaluated only when it is actually called with the parameter `n`, thus avoiding unnecessary calculations.

Another technique to improve performance in Haskell is the use of available high-level libraries. Haskell offers a wide range of libraries and frameworks optimized for various operations, such as numerical calculation, file parsing, string processing, etc. Using these libraries instead of implementing algorithms from scratch can lead to a considerable reduction in execution times and memory consumption.

An example of using a high-level library is the `vector` library for numerical calculation. This library offers efficient implementations of arrays and methods for data manipulation, allowing for writing more concise and performant code. Consider, for example, the following code that calculates the dot product between two vectors:

```
import qualified Data.Vector as V

dotProduct :: V.Vector Double -> V.Vector Double -> Double
dotProduct v1 v2 = V.sum (V.zipWith (*) v1 v2)
```

In this case, we use the functions provided by the `vector` library to efficiently execute the dot product.

Another technique to optimize performance in Haskell is the use of parallelism and concurrency techniques. Haskell offers support for lightweight concurrency through threads and parallel computation through the use of specific libraries such as `Control.Concurrent` and `Control.Parallel`. These techniques allow for making the most of system resources and executing operations in parallel to improve performance.

Consider, for example, the following code that calculates the sum of squares of the first n integers using parallelism:

```
import Control.Parallel

parSumSquares :: Int -> Int
parSumSquares n = s1 `par` (s1 + s2)
```

where

```
s1 = sum [x * x | x <- [1..n `div` 2]]
s2 = sum [x * x | x <- [(n `div` 2) + 1..n]]
```
```

In this case, the `par` function is used to evaluate the two sums `s1` and `s2` in parallel, improving overall performance.
```

Finally, another technique to optimize code in Haskell is the use of memoization techniques. Memoization involves storing the results of function calls to avoid recalculating them in the future. This can lead to a significant reduction in execution times for computationally expensive functions. Consider, for example, the following implementation of the Fibonacci sequence using memoization:

```
fib :: Int -> Integer
fib n = fibs !! n
  where
    fibs = 0 : 1 : zipWith (+) fibs (tail fibs)
```

In this case, the Fibonacci sequence is calculated by storing the results in a list, avoiding the recalculation of already computed values.

In conclusion, Haskell is a powerful language that offers many techniques to improve the performance of applications and optimize the code efficiently. By using lazy evaluation functions, high-level libraries, parallelism and concurrency techniques, and memoization, it is possible to write performant and efficient code in Haskell.

Index

1. Introduction pg.4

2. Installation of Haskell pg.15

3. Basic Syntax of Haskell pg.22

4. Types of data in Haskell pg.29

5. Haskell Functions pg.35

6. Haskell List Comprehension pg.44

7. Haskell Pattern Matching pg.49

8. Haskell Recursion pg.55

9. Advanced data types in Haskell pg.60

10. Higher-order functions Recursive functions in Haskell pg.66

11. Haskell Lambda Functions pg.73

12. Monads and Functional Programming pg.79

13. Examples of writing Hello World in Haskell pg.84

14. Lists in Haskell pg.88

15. Tuple in Haskell pg.94

16. Typeclasses in Haskell pg.100

17. Monads in Haskell pg.105

18. Functors in Haskell pg.112

19. Applications in Haskell pg.117

20. Error handling in Haskell pg.126

21. Inheritance in Haskell pg.133

22. Lazy evaluation pg.140

23. Performance and Optimization in Haskell pg.150

Copyright © 2024

www.ingramcontent.com/pod-product-compliance
Lightning Source LLC
Chambersburg PA
CBHW050100230526
45470CB00004B/1615